NOW YOU CAN READ...
MOSES THE LEADER

STORY RETOLD BY ROSALIND SUTTON

ILLUSTRATED BY RUSSELL LEE

Date Due

AUG 6 '88		
8/6/95		

Code 4386-04, CLS-4, Broadman Supplies, Nashville, Tenn., Printed in U.S.A.

648

THOMAS NELSON PUBLISHERS · NASHVILLE · CAMDEN · NEW YORK
Copyright © 1983 by Brimax Rights, Inc.

First Baptist Church
MEDIA LIBRARY

A boy called Moses lived in a great palace. It was the home of the king of Egypt. The king's daughter had looked after Moses since he was a baby. She had found Moses lying in a cradle. It was hidden in the bulrushes near the river. His mother had hidden him there. She was afraid of the cruel king. The king's name was Pharaoh.

Then a very strange thing happened. As Andy and the rest of the class looked on, Mrs. Applelarney began to shrink, and shrink, and shrink until finally she was no bigger than a bubble, herself!

"Oh dear. Suddenly I feel so light," she gasped, floating high above her desk.

Everyone's eyes were on Andy. He dipped the bubble wand back into the bottle. This time when he blew, two more bubbles came bouncing down the aisles, finally cozying up to the Cooper twins.

As everyone watched, Brian and Bradley Cooper turned into two little bubbly boys.

"Eeee . . . eee . . . ," they squealed with delight, floating hand in hand over the hamster cage.

"A most memorable show-and-tell, Andrew," commented Mrs. Applelarney, flying in front of the blackboard. Andy continued to blow bubbles from the old bottle until his classmates were all bouncing bubblelike around the room.

Finally Andy blew himself a bubble. Catching a breeze, he followed Mrs. Applelarney and the rest of the class out the window.

Once in the open air, the bubbly kindergarten class blew all the way to Andy's house.

"Over there is my swing set," Andy proudly told them. "And there's my sandbox."

Just then a gust of wind blew everyone higher into the sky.

"Fine day for a field trip, I suppose," Mrs. Applelarney said, trying to sound composed.

"If you look way, way down, you might be able to see my puppy, though he's kind of small," Andy sputtered, as a family of crows flew by.

"And if you look straight ahead, you'll be able to see an airplane—a very, very big airplane!" Andy gasped.

It was true. A big jet plane was zooming straight at them. When the pilot saw the bubbly group, he quickly steered below them.

"Looks like rain," Andy yelled. A big gray cloud lightly grazed their heads.

Suddenly drops of rain began to fall. The bubbles began to pop! Everyone tumbled down, down, down to the sand-box behind Andy's house.

"That's all the time we have for show-and-tell today,"
Mrs. Applelarney said, shaking the sand out of her hair.

On the way back to the classroom, Andy overheard Emma Oletti say, "I think Andy has the best show-and-tells in the class, maybe in the whole school. I wonder what he'll bring in next?"

Andy frowned. He had used up all the magic bubbles and didn't know what to bring for show-and-tell next time.

Suddenly, Mrs. Applelarney called him to the front of the line. "That certainly was an interesting show-and-tell, Andrew," she said, pulling a feather out of her hair. Andy shook his head and blushed with delight.

"But you know," she said, "next time, I'd prefer to see your fork again, if that would be all right."

The End

As she sat by a pool, the princess talked to Moses about his people. Many years ago, she said, Moses' people had to come to Egypt to look for food. The king had made them slaves. He made them work very hard.

When Moses became older, he went out to watch the slaves. They made bricks with clay and straw and water. The wet bricks dried in the hot sun. Pharaoh made the slaves build great cities. If they stopped to rest, his cruel soldiers hit them with whips. Moses was sad because his people were not free. One day he killed a soldier who was hitting one of his people. Pharaoh was very angry.

Moses left the palace. He went across the desert into another land. Many years passed. Moses became a shepherd. One day, as he was looking after his sheep on the hillside, God sent him a sign. Moses saw a bush in front of him. It burst into flames but the flames did not burn the bush.

A voice called to Moses. It came from the middle of the bush.

"Moses, take off your shoes and come near. This is holy ground." It was the voice of God.

Moses knelt before the burning bush. God told him to lead his people out of Egypt to a new land. They would be free. He told Moses to go back to Egypt and ask Pharaoh to let the people go.

Moses went back to Egypt. He found his brother Aaron. They called the slaves together to tell them what God had said.

The people bowed their heads and gave thanks to God.

Moses and Aaron went to the palace. They came before the king to tell him of God's words.

Pharaoh became very angry.

"Why should I listen to your God? I need slaves to work for me. I will never let them go!"

Pharaoh had his soldiers beat the slaves so they would work harder. God punished Pharaoh. He made Pharaoh's people and their animals sick. The king's people became afraid. They begged Pharaoh to let the slaves go.

"Go," Pharaoh said to Moses. "Take your children and your animals. Go from this land."

Moses helped his people make ready to leave. They tied things in bundles. Cattle and sheep were herded together. Their cooking pots and water jars were slung across oxen. They then made their way on foot, out of the land of Egypt. They had been slaves for more than four hundred years.

Moses led his people across the desert. There was little water or food. The children cried. They were hot and tired. The people were afraid.

"Do not be afraid," said Moses. "God will show us the way."

God did not forget them. By day, He sent a pillar of cloud in front of them. It showed them the way to go.

At night, a pillar of fire glowed in the dark, so that they could see.

In Egypt, people
were angry.
Without the slaves,
there was no one
to do the work.
Pharaoh sent all
his soldiers to
bring back
the slaves.

First Baptist Church
MEDIA LIBRARY

Moses and his people came to the Red Sea. They could not cross the sea. They said to Moses, "Why have you led us here to die?"

"God will help us," said Moses. God put a pillar of cloud between them and Pharaoh's army. The soldiers could not see them.

Then God said to Moses, "Lift your staff over the sea. The sea will part and leave a path in the middle. Your people can cross to the other side."

Moses did as he was told. There came a mighty wind. The sea rolled back.

Moses and his people crossed to
the other side. They saw Pharaoh's
men follow. What could they do?
They were lost.

God told Moses to stretch his hand over the sea. When he did so, the waves crashed like thunder. The waters of the sea came together. The sea covered the wicked soldiers. Not one was left.

Moses and his people fell onto
their knees to thank God. God had
saved them. They were free. At
last they were going to the land
God had given them.

All these appear in the pages of
the story. Can you find them?

Princess

Moses

Pharaoh

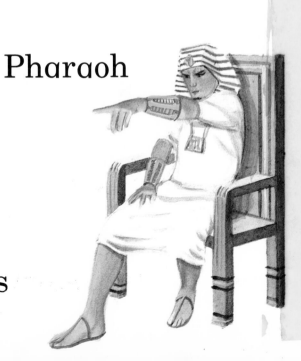

slaves